Strategic Warning &
The Role Of Intelligence

Sponsors	3
The CIA & Strategic Warning: The 1968 Soviet-Led Invasion of Czechoslovakia	5
Timeline	13
The Kremlin, the Prague Spring, and the Brezhnev doctrine	17
Declassified Intelligence Documents (selected excerpts)	25
Charting the Prague Spring	25
The Soviet-Czechoslovak Crisis Unfolds	33
Anticipating Surprise: The Soviets Invade	47
The Aftermath: Assessing Damage and Impact	55
Acknowledgements	65
DVD Contents	66

The Historical Collections Division (HCD) of CIA's Information Management Services is responsible for executing the Agency's Historical Review Program. This program seeks to identify, collect, and review for possible release to the public documents of significant historical importance.

The mission of HCD is to:

- Promote an accurate, objective understanding of the information and intelligence that has helped shape the foundation of major US policy decisions.

- Broaden access to lessons learned, presenting historical material to emphasize the scope and context of past actions.

- Improve current decision-making and analysis by facilitating reflection on the impacts and effects arising from past decisions.

- Uphold Agency leadership commitments to openness, while protecting the national security interests of the US.

- Provide the American public with valuable insight into the workings of the Government.

Lyndon B. Johnson Presidential Library and Museum

The Lyndon Baines Johnson Library and Museum is one of eleven presidential libraries administered by the National Archives and Records Administration. The Library houses 45 million pages of historical documents which include the papers from the entire public career of Lyndon Baines Johnson and also from those of close associates. These papers and the vast administrative files from the presidency are used primarily by scholars. The museum provides year-round public viewing of its permanent historical cultural exhibits. Special activities and exhibits are sponsored privately by the Friends of the LBJ Library and its parent organization, the LBJ Foundation.

The mission of the LBJ Library is to:

- Preserve and protect the historical materials in the collections of the Johnson Library and make them readily accessible;

- Increase public awareness of the American experience through relevant exhibitions and educational programs;

- Advance the Lyndon Baines Johnson Library and Museum's standing as a center for intellectual activity and community leadership while meeting the challenges of a changing world.

The CIA & Strategic Warning:

The 1968 Soviet-Led Invasion of Czechoslovakia

An Overview*

The Czechoslovak crisis, as it came to be known, started in January 1968, when Alexander Dubček was elevated to the post of First Secretary of the Communist Party of Czechoslovakia (CPCz), replacing moribund Antonin Novotny, who had served as First Secretary since 1957. Under Dubček, the communist leadership embarked on a program of dramatic liberalization of the Czechoslovak political, economic, and social order, including the overhaul of the CPCz leadership, increased freedom of speech, surrender of authority to the Czech National Assembly by the Communist Party, real elections at local and national levels, and even the suggestion of legalizing non-communist political parties.

In all, the crisis lasted more than a year, with the first nine months consisting of Czech reforms triggering Soviet statements of concern and eventually threats, buttressed by Warsaw Pact military buildups disguised as exercises *(see Czechoslovak Crisis Timeline for a complete chronology of events)*. When the invasion occurred in the early morning hours of 21 August, the Czechoslovak leadership was not immediately removed, but remained largely intact through April 1969, when Dubček was finally replaced as First Secretary by a more pro-Soviet Gustav Husak.

Dubček and the Prague Spring: A Threat to the Warsaw Pact?

All this alarmed Moscow and the leadership of the Warsaw Pact, but throughout the Prague Spring, Dubček went out of his way to demonstrate his personal loyalty to Moscow and Prague's intention to remain firmly within the Warsaw Pact military alliance. How sincere he was in these remonstrations is difficult to say, but Dubček and his allies clearly feared a repetition of the Hungarian uprising of 1956, brutally crushed by Soviet troops.

These fears were mirrored in Washington and, to a certain extent, even in Moscow. Certainly the Kremlin, under the nearly comatose leadership of Leonid Brezhnev, had no desire to provoke a crisis, while any disturbance anywhere was seen as a threat to the increasingly fragile stability of the Soviet bloc. There was, moreover, a general tendency—at least in the West—to view some kind of

---

* This overview is excerpted in large part from an essay by Donald P. Steury, CIA historian, entitled *Strategic Warning: The CIA and the Soviet Invasion of Czechoslovakia*.

internal reform as a necessary precondition for the stability of the Warsaw Pact.

Although the Pact had been created in 1955 as a "paper organization" to counter the rearming of West Germany and the cooperative effort of the Western allies in NATO, by the early 1960s the Warsaw Pact gradually was acquiring more form and substance as a military alliance. Under Khrushchev, the Pact had become the mechanism by which Moscow could introduce large-scale troop reductions, principally in conventional forces deployed to Europe. With substantially fewer forces on the ground in Eastern Europe, Moscow had more at stake in making the alliance work. Thus, although the non-Soviet members of the Warsaw Pact had little choice in joining the organization, once members of an alliance with the Soviet Union, they found they had a relatively greater voice in ordering their own affairs.

By 1965, the Warsaw Pact was becoming a framework in which the nations of Eastern Europe could exercise a growing level of autonomy. General disenchantment with Marxist economics and Soviet-style politics and the growing attraction of the West were giving the states of Eastern Europe "both the incentive and the opportunity for striking out on their own," noted the Office of National Estimates (ONE),

in a special memorandum in 1965. "The Soviets," according to ONE, would find it difficult to arrest the process; "though crises are an ever-present danger, we believe that these countries will be able successfully to assert their own national interests gradually and without provoking Soviet intervention." The Prague Spring thus seems to have been evaluated as part of a broader reform movement with the Warsaw Pact as a whole. There was the cautious belief that Sasha Dubček–if he were very careful and very, very lucky–just might pull it off.

CIA Analysis and the Prague Spring

Agency analysis in the Prague Spring focused in on two critical factors. This first of these was the importance of the Czechoslovak armed forces to Warsaw Pact military planning. In a war with NATO, the Czechoslovak army would have formed the first echelon of a Warsaw Pact attack into southern Germany, intended to outflank any NATO effort to defend along the inner-German border and, ultimately, to drive across Bavaria and Baden-Württemberg to the Rhein. The Czechoslovak military leadership was given command of the Front and would have retained command of its armed forces in wartime–which put Czechoslovakia, alongside Poland, in a privileged position in the Warsaw Pact hierarchy. The reduction of Soviet ground forces in the early 1960s had only increased the importance of the Czechoslovak army to Soviet/Warsaw Pact war planning.

The second factor was the importance of the Czechoslovak economy within the Soviet bloc. Czechoslovakia was among the most industrially developed of the Warsaw Pact countries, yet it had suffered the most from 20 years of communist rule.

In 1948, Czechoslovakia was better off than West Germany, but by 1968 per capita output had slipped to about two-thirds that of the Federal Republic, in addition to major differences in quality. Moscow was aware that popular opinion in Czechoslovakia blamed the old-line party hierarchy for its relative decline. "Economic pressure is a major force for political change in Eastern Europe," noted a March 1968 intelligence report. Without meaningful reform, Czechoslovakia's problems "may become acute in the next two or three years...."

To CIA, the Czechoslovak economic crisis meant that Soviet leaders were concerned over the stability and reliability of Prague's military contribution to the Warsaw Pact. They thus were likely to be receptive to anything that promised a solution to Czechoslovakia's internal problems. Moscow also realized that the first result of a premature attempt to decisively intervene in Czechoslovakia likely would be demoralization of the Czechoslovak military. At the same time, the Kremlin was concerned that the "contagion" of Czech democratization not spread nor that the Czechoslovaks themselves go too far in creating an open society. All these factors seemed to ad up to a Soviet decision to watch, wait, and hope for the best, while preparing for the worst.

Setting Limits on Reform

As the snows of winter melted, it became possible to hypothesize that Dubček's "socialism with a human face" would find a place in the Warsaw Pact. On 23 March, Czechoslovakia was the main topic of discussion at a Warsaw Pact summit in Dresden. CIA reported that Moscow had used the occasion to put a limit on how far Dubček could go, but that

> [i]f the new leadership in Prague proceeds carefully...good progress can be made....[I]n view of its political, economic and military importance to the USSR and the Soviet Bloc, the CSSR cannot start an anti-socialist or anti-Soviet policy. The USSR would not allow this...[but] there [is] no anti-socialist or anti-Soviet movement involved in the new political evolution of the CSSR...only a strong movement for democratization and liberalization of the system

Consequently, according to CIA, the Soviet leadership "...did not consider Dubček as someone willing to start an anti-Soviet line."

This conclusion was supported by the CPCz Party Action Program, published on 10 April. The Directorate of Intelligence (DI) noted that it was "restrained in tone, realistic and relatively free of cant... disappointing to the radical reformers in some aspects." Armed with this evidence of Dubček's moderation and the Kremlin's tolerance, by the end of April, the DI had concluded that the leaders of the Soviet Union appeared to have "grudgingly accepted" the Czechoslovak reforms. The only limits placed on these reforms were the continued primacy of the CPCz and that Czechoslovakia honor its military and economic commitments to the USSR. An unsigned CIA memorandum argued that the Soviets could have applied economic pressure, had they wanted to halt Dubček's reforms and cited as evidence a Czech radio broadcast:

> Let us not forget that...our cars run on Soviet gas, two out of three rolls are baked from Soviet flour, and our gigantic metallurgical combines would come to a standstill within a few days after Soviet ore shipments stopped. Nothing of the sort is happening

here, as is common knowledge: cars are running, rolls are baked, and so forth

Tensions Rise

In general, CIA analysis seems to have accurately characterized attitudes inside the Soviet Politburo. Correctly deducing that the Soviet leadership was split over the need for intervention, the Office of National Estimates reported that—at least for the time being—the Kremlin had accepted the Czech reforms as the lesser of two evils. Although there was strong evidence of Soviet "anxieties" over the Czech reforms, Dubček continued to prove himself to be adept at balancing reforms inside Czechoslovakia with continued adherence to doctrines of communism and pledges to uphold Czechoslovakia's military commitments to the Warsaw Pact. There thus seemed reason to hope that, although Soviet pressure on Czechoslovakia would increase over "the long hot summer," the Soviets would "take no 'harder,' i.e., military measures."

Relations between Moscow and Prague deteriorated steadily in the next few months. The Soviet Politburo remained reluctant to sanction military action, but CIA in late April reported that "[d]evelopments since the Dresden meeting indicate that the Russians and the Eastern Europeans were dissatisfied with the results of the conference and remained concerned about Czechoslovakia's course." By mid-June, Czechoslovakia was reported to be in an "uneasy truce" with Moscow. Dubček reportedly was now playing for time, hoping that he could implement enough reforms quickly to present the Kremlin leadership with a fait accompli. "At some stage in the game," the Agency reported, "the Soviets will...become aware that their earlier hopes for a return to anything like the status quo ante in Czechoslovakia were without foundation. It is the Czech hope that this realization will have come too late and that the Soviets' reactions will be minimal."

It was now clear to Agency analysts that the Politburo viewed developments in Czechoslovakia with growing unease. Indecision still reigned in Moscow, but the only thing preventing the Soviet Union from intervening militarily was concern over the broad impact of yet another violent repression of an Eastern European bid for autonomy. On 17 July, the Office of National Estimates warned CIA Director Helms: "We know of no way of foretelling the precise event in Czechoslovakia which might trigger...extreme Soviet reaction, or of foreseeing the precise circumstances which might produce within the Soviet leadership an agreement to move with force." But the Soviets believed that communist authority in Czechoslovakia was seriously threatened. "The possibility will exist for some time that the Soviets will choose to intervene rather than permit Czechoslovakia to...move decisively toward... an open disavowal of communism or of the Warsaw

Pact." Still, the Soviet leadership had not decided what to do. Very much still depended on Dubček and Czechoslovakia. "Some appropriate concessions" from Dubček would remove the need for military action. So would a conservative overthrow of Dubček.

The crisis seemed to be reaching a climax at the end of July, when Soviet leaders traveled to Cierna nad Tisou, on the Czechoslovak border, to meet with the Czech Politburo. The bilateral talks were cloaked in secrecy, but on 31 July the Soviet wire service TASS reported that the talks at Cierna had an atmosphere of "frankness and comradeship," which, according to CIA analysts, was Soviet code for tough talk but no action. Ominously, however, that same day Dubček's family was reported leaving Czechoslovakia for Yugoslavia.

The Cierna conference concluded on 1 August and was almost immediately followed by a general Warsaw Pact summit at Bratislava. Two days later the only written statement to emerge from either of these meetings was produced. It was little more than a statement of alliance solidarity, combined with an affirmation of the principles of Marxism-Leninism. With this, the crisis seemed to be over. The Czechoslovak leadership apparently had mollified its Soviet and Warsaw Pact allies, at least for the time being. Dubček seemed to have won.

Less than three weeks later the Soviet Union invaded Czechoslovakia.

CIA Military Reporting

As a member of the Warsaw Pact, Czechoslovakia was perforce under a fairly high level of routine surveillance. As tensions heightened over the spring and summer of 1968, so did the attention paid to Czechoslovakia by US and NATO intelligence services. The full panoply of sources available to Western intelligence included photo-reconnaissance satellites, covert intelligence collection performed by USAF aircraft transiting the Berlin traffic corridors (and by SR-71 reconnaissance aircraft along the inner German border), SIGINT collection sites in southern Germany and on the Teufelsberg in occupied Berlin, and–particularly important during the Czechoslovak crisis–observations by the Allied military missions in East Germany. There also appeared to have been some agent reporting available.

Military tensions ratcheted up in the last half of March, as the USSR concentrated troops along the Czech-East German border in the period leading up to the Warsaw Pact summit in Dresden. This was judged to be a preventative measure, but on 9 May CIA reported that Soviet troops in Poland had been seen south of Krakow moving in the direction of Czechoslovakia. Noting that the Soviets had a total of 39 divisions available, should they decide to intervene militarily, CIA concluded that "[i]t would appear that Moscow has decided to do some saber-rattling in order to influence the Czechoslovaks to put a brake on their democratization."

The next month, the Soviet Union began a series of Pact-wide military exercises designed to mask the build-up of forces against Czechoslovakia. These included:

- Sumava or Böhmerwald: over 20-30 June, a command post and communications exercise involving Soviet, East German, Czech, and Polish troops in Czechoslovakia.

- Niemen: from 23 July to 10 August, a rear-services exercise.

- Skyshield: an air defense exercise, conducted over 11-20 August.

Of the three, the rear services exercise was regarded as the most ominous, since it involved recalling reservists, requisitioning transport from the civilian economy, and mobilizing forces from Latvia to Ukraine—measures that obviously could be designed to cover the mass movement of troops against Czechoslovakia. Nevertheless, although CIA warned that these exercises could well be signs of military intervention, most analysts in the US intelligence community continued to believe that the Soviet Union would exercise restraint.

The situation grew more ominous in July. On 26 July, CIA reported that the Polish Government was under great pressure to prepare for an invasion. The Soviet 32nd Army in Poland had mobilized, as had large forces in East Germany. Five Polish divisions in the Silesian Military District were at a high state of readiness. That same day, substantial elements of three East German divisions moved into restricted areas 75 miles south of Berlin. To find out more, USAF SR-71s flew along the inner German border, from where they could monitor developments up to 100 KM inside East Germany.

By the end of the month, most of the Soviet troops in Czechoslovakia had been withdrawn, but they remained just outside the country and Western observers noted that the route signs leading into Czechoslovakia for the military movements had been left in place. Four Soviet divisions in Hungary were reported moving into the field, roadblocks were set up and convoys were seen moving in the direction of Czechoslovakia. The Soviet air forces on

31 July were detected making contingency preparations for operations in Czechoslovakia, while high-level military officials in Moscow were reported operating on an indefinite alert status. Three days later, CIA's Office of Strategic Research (OSR) warned, "[i]t would appear the Soviet high command has in about two weeks' time completed military preparations sufficient for intervening in Czechoslovakia if that is deemed necessary by the political leadership."

CIA Warning and the Czech Invasion

Over the next three weeks, CIA was forced to function without the support of its principal collection asset, photo-reconnaissance satellites. The film-return systems in use at the time lacked the flexibility to respond to the rapidly changing situation in Czechoslovakia. A KH-4B satellite was in orbit, but its canister was not recovered until after the invasion. When it was, the film showed Soviet forces deployed to invade—airfields packed with aircraft, Soviet military vehicles painted with white crosses to distinguish them from identical Czech equipment.

By this point in time, however, overhead reconnaissance was not really necessary; there already was ample intelligence from other sources to show that, by the end of July, the Warsaw Pact was mobilized for an invasion of Czechoslovakia.

The next two weeks or so were something of an anti-climax, for the simple reason that the Soviets themselves had not decided to intervene. This hesitation gave some reason to hope that an invasion was not forthcoming—but, with nearly 40 Soviet divisions on the move, it was clear the Soviet alert remained in place. When the Soviets did decide on 18 August to intervene, it was announced by SIGINT reporting of a Soviet military communications blackout all over Central Europe.

Two days later, on the morning of the invasion, Director of Central Intelligence Richard Helms met with Bruce Clarke (Director of Strategic Research in the DI) and Richard Lehman (the DI's Director of Current Intelligence) for an update on the Czechoslovak situation. Lehman relayed a wire service report that Soviet leaders had been summoned to Moscow for an urgent Politburo meeting—which, in fact, had occurred on 18 August. This was unusual in itself: Soviet leaders normally spent August entrenched in their dachas, and only a crisis would suffice to get them out. Clarke, Lehman, and Helms agreed that, taken together with the military alert in Central Europe, the emergency Politburo meeting was a sure indicator something was about to happen, most probably the invasion of Czechoslovakia. Helms was already scheduled to meet with President Johnson and decided to convey the information personally. Remarkably, LBJ rejected that conclusion, saying, "Dick, that Moscow meeting is to talk about us." What Johnson knew, and Helms did not know, was that the Soviet Union and the United States were due to make a joint announcement on 21 August concerning the planned strategic arms limitation talks. Not unreasonably, but unfortunately, LBJ believed that to be the subject of the meeting in the Kremlin.

The President and his advisers soon were disabused of that notion. At 2300, central European time, on 20 August, a Soviet special forces battalion landed at and occupied Prague airport. At 2311 NATO radar monitors reported that the air space around Prague was covered with artificial "snow," blanking out radar screens and preventing observation of what was happening. Just a few hours later, at 2200, EDT, Helms was summoned back to the White House for an emergency meeting. The invasion of Czechoslovakia was underway. Given the swiftness of events, it is hard to see how Johnson could have received more warning than he did. Official Washington was holding its breath in August 1968, waiting to see what the Soviets would do. Ample, precise, and accurate strategic warning concerning events in Eastern Europe had been pouring in all summer. The August calm before the storm may have meant that much of the intelligence community was surprised by the invasion when it occurred, but there had been no indication that the Soviets had stood down in Eastern Europe, nor had strategic warning ever been withdrawn.

A CIA memorandum prepared immediately after the invasion noted that the decision to intervene must have come very late in the game. Exactly how and when Moscow's forbearance "became unraveled" was something of a mystery. To CIA analysts, however, it was clear that the decision had come sometime after the Cierna nad Tiscu and Bratislava conferences. The time that elapsed, the scattering

of the Soviet leadership to their dachas for the August holidays, the attitude of the Soviet press, the anodyne communiques that were issued after each meeting all were indicators that the Dubček government was being given more time—to do what was not clear. "The mostly likely explanation," Agency analysts concluded, "appears to be that, under the impact of internal pressures within the leadership and of importuning from its anxious allies in Eastern Europe...the fragile balance in the Soviet leadership which produced the Cierna agreement has, in the space of less than three weeks, been upset in favor of those who may all along have wanted the toughest kind of policy...." With the political scales in Moscow in such precarious balance, "it would not have needed a great shock to upset them."

And so, in the early morning hours of 21 August, Czechoslovakia was invaded from the north, east, and south by 20 Warsaw Pact divisions totaling some 250,000 men. At the same time, the positions vacated by these units were backfilled by 10 Soviet divisions. Once strategic points in Czechoslovakia were occupied, most of these forces redeployed into western Czechoslovakia, restoring the front against NATO. There they were backed by the full might of the Warsaw Pact, including thousands of nuclear weapons targeted against Western and Central Europe. Nothing short of a world war was likely to get them out. In 1938, the Western powers had responded to threats against Czechoslovakia by backing down, rather than face a Nazi Germany they falsely believed was ready for war. In 1968 they had no choice.

Note: This essay, complete with footnotes, appears on the DVD.

CZECHOSLOVAK
Crisis Timeline
January – August 1968

MARCH

Dubček and Czech leaders attend Warsaw Pact meeting in Dresden. Czechoslovaks urged to be cautious in the implementation of reforms.

Soviet leader Leonid Brezhnev issues warnings against imperialist subversion of communist countries. First Soviet steps in mobilizing support for intervention in Czechoslovakia.

JUNE

Soviet troop movements reported along Czech border. Soviet troops in East Germany move southward.

Soviet Army delegation visits Czechoslovakia.

The Soviet Union notifies the Johnson Administration of its renewed interest in SALT talks.

Soviet Premier Kosygin and Defense Minister Grechko visit Prague accompanied by commanders of Soviet forces that have taken up positions on Czech border.

First Warsaw Pact troops enter Czechoslovakia for maneuvers scheduled to begin 20 June.

Warsaw Pact maneuvers formally end. Soviet troops remain in Czechoslovakia.

APRIL

Action Program of reforms adopted by Czech Central Committee.

MAY

Dubček, Smrkovsky, and Cernik meet with Soviet leaders in Moscow.

Leaders of Warsaw Pact countries (excluding Czechoslovakia and Romania) convene in Moscow. No communique is issued.

JULY

Radio Moscow increases its daily broadcasts to Czechoslovakia. Secretary of State Rusk denies rumors that the US warned the USSR against military intervention in Czechoslovakia.

Moscow announces large rear service exercise to take place in western USSR. Czechoslovak military officials state 5,000 to 6,000 Soviet troops remain in country. An estimated 2,000 Soviet troops are reported encamped at Zilina, Czechoslovakia.

Soviets announce large air defense exercise over a broad area of USSR.

Meeting of Czech and Soviet Party leaders in Cierna nad Tisou begins.

CZECHOSLOVAKIA CRISIS TIMELINE
JANUARY – AUGUST 1968

Moscow announces rear services exercise has been extended to East Germany and Poland. US embassy in Warsaw receives reports of Soviet troops moving into Poland from the USSR. More Soviet troops move into East Germany.

US attache sees two large Soviet convoys in central Czechoslovakia. Soviet forces in Hungary move into assembly areas. East German and Polish reserves are reportedly called up.

Soviets conduct air defense exercise (Operation Skyshield) over large part of western USSR.

Brezhnev, Kosygin, and Podgorniy return from vacation early to attend an emergency meeting of the Politburo.

LBJ receives a letter from Kosygin proposing that the President announce, on 21 August, that US-Soviet arms limitation talks will be held in Leningrad on 30 September.

Warsaw Pact troops cross border into Czechoslovakia. Ruzyne Airport near Prague is occupied by Soviet airborne troops.

Western leaders are informed of the Soviet invasion through their respective Soviet ambassadors. President Johnson calls an emergency meeting of the National Security Council.

AUGUST

Czech leaders return to Prague and assure citizens that an understanding has been reached with the Soviets.

Soviet press ceases its attacks on Czechoslovakia.

Czechoslovak leaders meet with Warsaw Pact leaders in Bratislava. A joint communique is issued.

The remaining troops from the June Warsaw Pact exercise leave Czechoslovakia. Decreased fear of intervention is evident throughout the Johnson Administration following the Bratislava meeting.

Most Soviet Politburo members leave Moscow and vacation near the Black Sea.

Additional troops enter the major cities and countryside of Czechoslovakia. They occupy Central Committee HQs and Prague radio station. Dubček and other party leaders are arrested.

Soviet news agency Tass issues a statement on the invasion that includes an unsigned letter requesting Soviet military assistance, purportedly from Czechoslovak officials.

Czech Party Presidium issues a statement that condemns the invasion of their country and denies that any Czechoslovak official requested Soviet military assistance.

Johnson condemns invasion in televised speech.

THE KREMLIN, THE PRAGUE SPRING, AND THE BREZHNEV DOCTRINE

BY MARK KRAMER
PROFESSOR, HARVARD UNIVERSITY

Until the late 1980s, the Soviet Union's determination to preserve Communism in East-Central Europe was not in doubt. When Communist regimes in Eastern Europe came under violent threat in the 1950s—in East Germany in 1953 and Hungary in 1956—Soviet troops intervened to subdue those challenges. A very different problem arose in 1968, when Czechoslovakia embarked on a dramatic, but entirely peaceful, attempt to change both the internal complexion of Communism and many of the basic structures of Soviet-East European relations. This eight-month-long experiment, widely known as the "Prague Spring," came to a decisive end in August 1968, when hundreds of thousands of Soviet and Warsaw Pact troops invaded Czechoslovakia.

Neither the Soviet Union nor Czechoslovakia exists any longer, but the legacy of the Prague Spring and the Soviet invasion is still being felt. The reforms that took place in Czechoslovakia in 1968 under the leadership of Alexander Dubček offered the first opportunity for an East European Communist regime to earn genuine popular support. Moscow's unwillingness to tolerate those reforms ensured that, from then on, stability in the Eastern bloc could be preserved only by the threat of another Soviet invasion.

That threat sufficed to hold the bloc together for more than twenty years, even when tested by severe crises like the one in Poland in 1980-1981. But soon after Mikhail Gorbachev came along and was no longer willing to use military force in Eastern Europe, the whole Soviet bloc collapsed. Because of the legacy of 1968, all the East European regimes still lacked the legitimacy they would have needed to sustain themselves without Soviet military backing. The invasion of Czechoslovakia saved Soviet-style Communism in Eastern Europe for more than two decades, but it could not forestall the eventual demise of the bloc.

This paper draws on recently declassified archival materials and memoirs to provide a reassessment of the 1968 crisis, showing how the confrontation with Czechoslovakia fit into Soviet policy toward Eastern Europe. The paper begins by discussing the context of the 1968 crisis, highlighting trends in Soviet policy in the late 1950s and 1960s. It then turns to the Prague Spring itself, explaining why the bold changes in Czechoslovakia provoked such a harsh reaction in Moscow. Finally, the chapter explores the international and domestic consequences of the Soviet-led invasion, focusing in particular on the promulgation of the "Brezhnev Doctrine," which set the tone for

Soviet-East European relations for the next 21 years.

CONTEXT OF THE 1968 CRISIS

From November 1956, when Soviet troops crushed a popular uprising in Hungary, to January 1968, when the Prague Spring began, Soviet-East European relations underwent several notable changes. Some developments facilitated greater Soviet control over Eastern Europe and better cohesion among the Warsaw Pact states, but numerous other factors tended to weaken Soviet control and to create fissures within the Eastern bloc.

Sources of Cohesion

From the early 1960s on, the Soviet Union sought to invigorate the Council for Mutual Economic Assistance (CMEA), which had been largely dormant since it was created by Stalin in 1949. Both Nikita Khrushchev and Leonid Brezhnev hoped to use the CMEA as a means of formally integrating the Soviet and East European economies. The "Basic Principles of Socialist Economic Integration," announced by Khrushchev with much fanfare in 1961, did not yield many results in the end; but the Soviet Union was able to exploit its economic preponderance to promote bilateral integration with each of the CMEA member-states, especially in trade relations. The unusually large proportion of foreign trade that the East European countries conducted with the Soviet Union and with other CMEA members rose to nearly 70 percent in the 1960s, except in the case of Romania. This trend did not bring the supranational integration that Soviet leaders had envisaged, but it did ensure that the East European states remained crucially dependent on (and therefore beholden to) the Soviet Union for key economic goods, particularly energy supplies.

The Soviet Union also fostered greater intra-bloc cohesion in the military sphere, a policy reflected in the newly emerging concept of "coalition warfare." This approach, as described in a classified report by Soviet military planners in the mid-1960s, called for a rapid, massive offensive against the North Atlantic Treaty Organization (NATO) by a combination of Soviet and East European forces using both nuclear and conventional weaponry:

> The defense strategy of the socialist countries must focus on seizing the most important regions and lines, and on absolutely preventing an incursion by the adversary's forces into the territory of the socialist countries. The strategy will be based on nuclear strikes in conjunction with the use of conventional firepower and mobile operations by combined forces, and also on the wide-scale use of obstruction.

To underscore the new emphasis on joint military operations, Soviet leaders took several steps to improve the capacity of East European troops to perform effectively alongside Soviet forces. With Moscow's backing, all the East European states significantly modernized and expanded their armies in the 1960s; and they made renewed efforts to promote the interoperability and standardization of Warsaw Pact armaments. From October 1962 on, the Soviet Union conducted joint military exercises with the East European armies. As a result, the

Warsaw Pact, which had been little more than a paper organization for several years after it was founded in 1955, finally started to acquire a few of the trappings of a real alliance.

These efforts to strengthen the Warsaw Pact were initiated by Khrushchev, but they were given even greater emphasis by Brezhnev. Unlike Khrushchev, who had sought to cut Soviet conventional forces and to rely predominantly on long-range nuclear missiles, Brezhnev committed the Soviet Union to a full-scale military buildup that expanded both conventional and nuclear weapons. The growth and modernization of Soviet conventional forces during the Brezhnev era facilitated major improvements in Soviet combat units in Eastern Europe, whose role was to serve as the "main strategic echelon" of the Warsaw Pact.

The increased vigor of the Pact helped to shore up the Soviet Union's position in Eastern Europe by allowing more of the financial costs of "defending the socialist commonwealth" to be passed off onto the East European governments while avoiding any commensurate change in the way the alliance operated. All the Soviet-dominated structures of the Warsaw Pact were preserved. Wartime control of allied forces was retained by the Soviet High Command, and even in peacetime the Pact's joint military exercises were infrequently—and then only symbolically—under the command of East European generals. Moreover, all the top posts in the Pact's Joint Command were still reserved exclusively for Soviet officers.

Soviet hegemony in the Warsaw Pact was further strengthened in the early to mid-1960s by a series of top-secret bilateral agreements providing for the deployment of Soviet tactical nuclear warheads and nuclear-capable delivery vehicles on the territory of East Germany, Poland, Czechoslovakia, and Hungary. The agreements were described as coming "within the framework of the Warsaw Pact," but all nuclear warheads were kept under strict Soviet control, and the dual-capable delivery vehicles that the East European countries possessed would have come under direct Soviet command if they had ever been equipped with nuclear warheads during a crisis. Moreover, the thousands of tactical nuclear weapons deployed by Soviet forces on East European territory were not subject to any sort of "dual-key" arrangement analogous to the procedures adopted by NATO in the mid-1960s to give the West European governments an effective veto over the use of American tactical nuclear weapons. Whenever Warsaw Pact exercises included combat techniques for nuclear warfare (as they routinely did from early 1962 on), all decisions on whether to "go nuclear" were reserved exclusively for Soviet political leaders and military commanders. East European leaders were not even consulted. Despite efforts by Romania and one or two other East-bloc governments in the 1960s to establish some form of nuclear "sharing" within the Warsaw Pact, the East European states were never given any say in the use of the alliance's "joint" nuclear arsenal.

The growth of Soviet strategic nuclear power in the 1960s also helped to strengthen Moscow's sphere of influence in Eastern Europe. Even at the time of the Hungarian revolution in 1956, when the Soviet Union's only means of delivering a nuclear attack against the continental United States was a limited number of long-range bombers, U.S. intelligence officials warned President Dwight Eisenhower that any steps aimed at "preparing for military intervention" in Hungary "would materially increase the risk of general war," including the possibility of a nuclear exchange. With the advent of Sputnik in October 1957 and the USSR's subsequent deployments of intercontinental ballistic missiles (ICBMs), as well as the expansion of the Soviet heavy bomber force, the Soviet Union by the early to mid-1960s clearly had the capacity to wreak untold destruction upon the

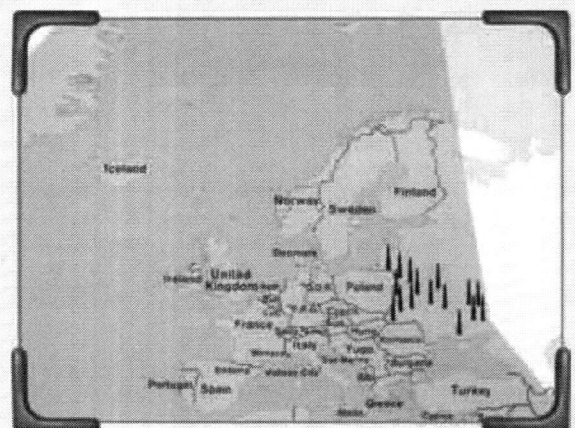

U.S. homeland. Although Soviet strategic nuclear forces at the time still lagged well behind those of the United States, the important thing, as was shown by President John F. Kennedy's overwhelming desire to avoid a nuclear exchange during the 1962 Cuban missile crisis, was that Soviet ICBMs could now inflict "unacceptable damage" on the United States. This new capability reinforced the pattern that emerged as early as June 1953, when the threat of Soviet nuclear or conventional retaliation against Western Europe helped deter NATO from coming to the defense of East German workers who had risen up en masse against the Communist regime. The much more dire consequences from any potential nuclear confrontation with the Soviet Union by the mid-1960s led U.S. Secretary of State Dean Rusk to acknowledge that "our capacity to influence events and trends within the Communist world is very limited. But it is our policy to do what we can...." Notions of "rollback" and "liberation" had been fanciful even in the 1950s, but they were all the more irrelevant by the mid- to late 1960s.

In the political sphere, as with the drive for economic integration and closer military relations, the Soviet Union accorded high priority to the goal of increased Soviet-East European cohesion. That goal was strongly endorsed by East European leaders who had come to be key figures in the 1960s, notably Władysław Gomułka of Poland and Walter Ulbricht of the German Democratic Republic (GDR). The Soviet Union's firm backing for Ulbricht during the severe crises of the late 1950s and early 1960s, when deepening economic strains and a large-scale exodus of East German citizens to West Berlin and the Federal Republic of Germany (FRG) had raised doubts about the very existence of the GDR, was crucial in preserving East Germany's frontline role in the Warsaw Pact. In particular, Khrushchev's decision to permit the building of the Berlin Wall in August 1961 halted the mass efflux of refugees from the GDR, staved off a further deterioration of the East German economy, and allowed the East German Communist party (formally known as the Socialist Unity Party of Germany, or SED) to reassert tight control in the GDR.

Soviet relations with Poland and East Germany remained a top priority in Moscow after Brezhnev took office. Brezhnev's chief foreign policy adviser in the 1960s, Andrei Aleksandrov-Agentov, recalled that the Soviet leader "greatly admired and respected" Gomułka and Ulbricht, and that Brezhnev, in turn, "acquired vast authority among the leaders of the other socialist states." As both Ulbricht and Gomułka encountered daunting political challenges at home in the latter half of the 1960s, they looked increasingly to Brezhnev for support against their domestic rivals, a trend that gave the USSR even greater influence in Poland and East Germany. (The unequal nature of these relationships became painfully evident when Brezhnev withdrew his backing for Gomułka and Ulbricht at the beginning of the 1970s, and both were quickly ousted.)

The USSR's hegemonic position in Eastern Europe was further enhanced by a highly publicized conference in Moscow in November 1960, which brought together high-level officials from 81 of the world's Communist parties and reaffirmed the "universally recognized vanguard role" of the

Communist Party of the Soviet Union (CPSU) in the international Communist movement. East European party leaders worked closely with Soviet officials at the conference to ensure that the participants would support Moscow's calls for increased "unity" and "solidarity" with the CPSU in the "stand against imperialism." Much the same was true of a subsequent all-European conference of Communist parties, held in Karlovy Vary in April 1967, a few years after Brezhnev had replaced Khrushchev. The conference was notable mainly for its continuity in emphasizing the USSR's preeminent role in European Communism.

Sources of Friction

Despite these signs of greater Soviet-East European cohesion, most developments during the early Brezhnev years pointed not toward an increase of Soviet control in Eastern Europe, but toward a loosening of that control. In part, this trend reflected the growing heterogeneity of the East European

societies, but it also was due to the schism in world Communism that had been opened by the Sino-Soviet conflict. A bitter split between the two leading Communist powers, stemming from genuine policy and ideological differences as well as from a personal clash between Khrushchev and Mao Zedong, developed behind-the-scenes in the late 1950s. The dispute intensified in June 1959, when the Soviet Union abruptly terminated its secret nuclear weapons cooperation agreement with China. Khrushchev's highly publicized visit to the United States in September 1959 further

antagonized the Chinese, and a last-ditch meeting between Khrushchev and Mao in Beijing right after Khrushchev's tour of the United States failed to resolve any of the major issues dividing the two sides. From then on, Sino-Soviet relations steadily deteriorated.

By the time Brezhnev took office in October 1964, the Sino-Soviet split had become a central feature of world politics, with important consequences for Soviet-East European relations. All the East European Communist leaders had learned of the rift in June 1960, when Soviet and Chinese officials attending the Romanian Communist Party's congress traded polemics and recriminations. Over the next several months, as news of the conflict spread throughout the world, Khrushchev and Mao made a few additional attempts to reconcile their differences; but the split, if anything, grew even wider. The ascendance of Brezhnev failed to ameliorate the situation. Initially, a few officials on both sides hoped that the change of leadership in Moscow would permit the two countries to achieve at least a partial rapprochement and to restore a semblance of unity in the international Communist movement, but those hopes proved illusory. Enmity between the two sides intensified and moved ever closer toward an armed clash.

The spill-over from the Sino-Soviet conflict into Eastern Europe was evident almost immediately, as the Soviet Union and China vied with one another for the backing of foreign Communist parties. In late 1960 and early 1961 the Albanian leader, Enver

Hoxha, sparked a crisis with the Soviet Union by openly aligning his country with China, a precedent that caused alarm in Moscow. Quite apart from the symbolic implications of Hoxha's move, Soviet leaders had always regarded Albania as an important member of the Warsaw Pact because of "its superb strategic location on the Mediterranean Sea." The rift with Yugoslavia in 1948 had eliminated the only other possible outlet for the Soviet Navy in the region. To ensure that Albania could serve as a full-fledged "military base on the Mediterranean Sea for all the socialist countries," the Soviet Union had been providing extensive weaponry, equipment, and training to the Albanian army and navy. In particular, the Albanian navy had received a fleet of twelve modern attack submarines, which initially were under Soviet control but were gradually being transferred to Albanian jurisdiction. Khrushchev believed that the submarines would allow Albania to pose a "serious threat to the operations of the NATO military bloc on the Mediterranean Sea," and thus he was dismayed to find that Soviet efforts to establish a naval bulwark on the Mediterranean might all have been for naught.

As soon as the rift with Albania emerged, the Soviet Union imposed strict economic sanctions, withdrew all Soviet technicians and military advisers, took back eight of the twelve submarines, dismantled Soviet naval facilities at the Albanian port of Vlorë, and engaged in bitter polemical exchanges with Albanian leaders. Khrushchev also ordered Soviet warships to conduct maneuvers along the Albanian coast, and he secretly encouraged pro-Moscow rivals of Hoxha in the Albanian Labor Party to carry out a coup. The coup attempt was rebuffed, and the other means of coercion proved insufficient to get rid of Hoxha or to bring about a change of policy. In December 1961, Khrushchev severed diplomatic relations with Albania and excluded it from both the Warsaw Pact and CMEA. However, he was not willing to undertake a full-scale invasion to bring Albania back within the Soviet orbit, not least because of logistical problems and the likelihood of confronting stiff armed resistance. The "loss" of Albania, though trivial compared to the earlier split with Yugoslavia and the deepening rift with China, marked the second time since 1945 that the Soviet sphere of influence in East-Central Europe had been breached.

To make matters worse, Soviet leaders soon discovered that China was secretly attempting to induce other East European countries to follow Albania's lead. At a closed plenum of the CPSU Central Committee in December 1963, a high-ranking Soviet official responsible for intra-bloc relations, Yurii Andropov, who became head of the Soviet State Security Committee (KGB) in 1967, noted that the Chinese had been focusing their efforts on Poland, Hungary, and East Germany:

> The Chinese leaders are carrying out a policy of crude sabotage in relation to Poland, Hungary, and the GDR. Characteristic of this is the fact that in September of this year, during conversations with a Hungarian official in China, Politburo member Chu De declared that China would welcome it if the Hungarian comrades diverged from the CPSU's line. But, Chu De threatened, if you remain on the side of the revisionists, we will have to take a stance against you.

China's efforts to lure these three countries (and possibly others) away from Soviet control à la Albania bore little fruit in the end, but Soviet leaders

obviously could not be sure of that at the time. The very fact that China was seeking to foment discord within the Soviet bloc was enough to spark consternation in Moscow.

The growing unease in Moscow about the effect of the Sino-Soviet split in Eastern Europe was piqued still further when Romania began to embrace foreign and domestic policies in the 1960s that were at times sharply at odds with the Soviet Union's own policies. Initially, the Romanian quest for autonomy was inspired by the USSR's attempts in 1961 to mandate a supranational economic integration program for CMEA, which would have relegated Romania to being little more than a supplier of agricultural goods and raw materials for the more industrialized Communist countries. In response, Romania began shifting much of its foreign trade away from CMEA toward the West and the Third World. In April 1964, the Romanian government issued a stinging rejection of the Soviet scheme. From then on, the reorientation of Romanian foreign trade gathered pace. By the late 1960s, Romania's trade with other CMEA countries as a proportion of its total foreign trade had dropped from 70 to just 45 percent.

Before long, Romania's defiance extended from economic matters into foreign policy and military activities as well. Romania staked out a conspicuously neutral position in the Sino-Soviet dispute, refusing to endorse Moscow's polemics or to join in other steps aimed at isolating Beijing from the rest of the Communist bloc. In 1967, Romania became the first East European country to establish diplomatic ties with West Germany, a step that infuriated East German leaders. That same year, the Romanians refused to attend the Karlovy Vary conference and maintained full diplomatic relations with Israel after the other Warsaw Pact countries had broken off all ties in the wake of the June 1967 Middle East War.

More important, Romania adopted an independent military doctrine of "Total People's War for the Defense of the Homeland," as well as a national military command structure entirely separate from that of the Warsaw Pact. Several years earlier, in 1958, the Romanian government had requested and obtained the withdrawal of all Soviet troops from Romania, but in the mid-1960s the new Romanian leader, Nicolae Ceauşescu, went much further by prohibiting joint Warsaw Pact maneuvers on Romanian territory and sending only token forces to participate in allied exercises elsewhere. Ceauşescu also stopped sending Romanian army officers to Soviet military academies for training and began openly challenging Soviet domination of the Warsaw Pact's military command structures. When the Soviet-Romanian treaty of friendship and cooperation came up for renewal in 1967-1968, Ceauşescu insisted that provisions be added to ensure that Romanian troops would be used only in Europe and only against "imperialist" countries, not against other Communist states. (Ceauşescu was thinking of China when he first proposed these amendments, but the provisions ended up being just as relevant to operations against Czechoslovakia.) Soviet leaders strongly resisted Ceauşescu's demands, but ultimately gave in. Although Romania had never been a crucial member of the Warsaw Pact,

Ceaușescu's growing recalcitrance on military affairs and foreign policy posed serious complications for the cohesion of the alliance.

Developments outside the Communist bloc also contributed to the loosening of Soviet control in Eastern Europe. The perceived threat of German aggression, which had long unified the Warsaw Pact governments, had gradually diminished. In the mid-1960s, West Germany had launched its Ostpolitik campaign to increase economic and political contacts in Eastern Europe, a campaign whose potentially disruptive impact on the Soviet bloc was well recognized in Moscow. As far back as November 1956, senior officials in the CPSU Central Committee apparatus had expressed strong misgivings about the effect that conciliatory overtures from the FRG might have on Poland and Czechoslovakia in the wake of the Hungarian revolution. They warned that if circumstances went too far, Poland "would no longer be interested in hosting Soviet troops" and that both Czechoslovakia and Poland might "pursue neutrality." That notion seemed far-fetched at the time, no matter how much West German policy might change; but by the mid- to late 1960s, as the FRG's Ostpolitik gathered pace, those earlier warnings seemed all too plausible.

Soviet policy in Eastern Europe also was increasingly constrained by the improvement in U.S.-Soviet relations that occurred after leaders on both sides recognized how close they had come to war during the Cuban missile crisis in October 1962. The new relationship was symbolized by the signing of the Limited Nuclear Test Ban Treaty in August 1963. The incipient superpower détente raised hopes in Moscow that strategic nuclear arms control agreements and increased economic ties would be forthcoming. Such prospects gave the Soviet leadership an incentive to proceed cautiously in Eastern Europe before taking actions that would undermine the détente and provoke Western retaliation (though the escalating U.S. military involvement in Vietnam presumably had the opposite effect). The advent of a more cooperative U.S.-Soviet relationship even spawned fears in Europe, both West and East, that the superpowers might eventually seek a formal condominium at the expense of the Europeans. Although this concern was especially acute in East Germany (where Ulbricht constantly worried that the Soviet Union might cut a deal over his head), similar anxieties were present in almost all of the East European countries.

Note: The complete article, with footnotes, appears on the DVD.

DECLASSIFIED
Intelligence Documents

Charting the
Prague Spring

~~SECRET~~
~~NO FOREIGN DISSEM~~

CENTRAL INTELLIGENCE AGENCY

OFFICE OF NATIONAL ESTIMATES

12 January 1968

SPECIAL MEMORANDUM NO. 1-68

SUBJECT: Czechoslovakia: A New Direction*

SUMMARY

The demotion of Czechoslovakia's Party First Secretary, Antonin Novotny, after 14 years in his post, signifies more than a change of personalities. A European Communist state is becoming less Communist and more European, and neither the pace nor the goals of the transition are likely to please Moscow. The forces which succeeded in removing Novotny -- presumably against the desires of the Soviets -- are now beginning to place emphasis not only on

---

* This memorandum was produced solely by CIA. It was prepared by the Office of National Estimates and coordinated with the Office of Current Intelligence.

~~S-E-C-R-E-T~~
~~NO FOREIGN DISSEM~~

~~GROUP 1
Excluded from automatic
downgrading and
declassification~~

economic reforms but political reforms as well. The latter will pertain mainly to domestic affairs -- the reduction of arbitrary party authority -- but also, inevitably, to foreign affairs. The new forces in Prague are concerned with internal political pluralism, as are the Yugoslavs, and with national sovereignty, as are the Romanians.

~~SECRET~~
No Foreign ~~Dissem~~/Background ~~Use~~ Only
No Dissem Abroad/Controlled ~~Dissem~~

CENTRAL INTELLIGENCE AGENCY
Directorate of Intelligence
23 April 1968

INTELLIGENCE MEMORANDUM

Czechoslovakia in Transition

Summary

Alexander Dubcek's beliefs that domestic repression must cease and that the time has come for Czechoslovakia to take its place in the family of nations have led to a bloodless but nevertheless very real revolution in Czechoslovakia. The unbending and unimaginative leadership of Antonin Novotny has been supplanted by a new administration dedicated to policies based on Dubcek's ideas. These include protection of the rights of the individual, the rule of law, a foreign policy serving the genuine interests of the country, and broad economic reforms. The party has promised to institutionalize such changes at a measured pace.

Dubcek still is faced with significant domestic opposition as distinct conservative and progressive factions have now emerged in the party. There is no reason to believe that he will, or safely could, renege on his promises for changes, though he probably will find it difficult in some instances to move ahead as directly and rapidly as he might desire.

Note: This memorandum was produced solely by CIA. It was prepared by the Office of Current Intelligence and coordinated with the Office of Economic Research, the Office of Strategic Research, the Office of National Estimates, and the Clandestine Services.

No ~~Dissem Abroad~~/Controlled Dissem
No Foreign Dissem/Background ~~Use~~ Only
~~SECRET~~

~~SECRET~~
~~No Foreign Dissem~~/Background Use Only
No Dissem Abroad/~~Controlled Dissem~~

The leaders of the Soviet Union appear to have conceded, though grudgingly, the Czechoslovak party's right to reform itself and to attempt a Communist "democratization." Brezhnev and Kosygin and the leaders of the Eastern European states nevertheless obviously fear the spread of such concepts to their own countries. The only limits placed on the new Czechoslovak regime by Moscow, however, are insistence that the Communist Party retain primacy, and that Czechoslovakia honor its commitments to the USSR, the other Communist states, and the international Communist movement. Dubcek has agreed, but the manner in which he and the Russians interpret these limits is certain to be a constant source of friction.

~~No Dissem Abroad~~/Controlled Dissem
No Foreign Dissem/Background ~~Use Only~~
~~SECRET~~

Approved For Release 2006/12/11 : CIA-RDP79R00967A000800010004-9

S-E-C-R-E-T

CENTRAL INTELLIGENCE AGENCY
OFFICE OF NATIONAL ESTIMATES

13 June 1968

SPECIAL MEMORANDUM NO. 12-68

SUBJECT: Czechoslovakia: The Dubcek Pause*

1. The related crises in internal Czechoslovak politics and in Soviet-Czechoslovak relations seem to have eased -- at home, into a delicate and perhaps temporary domestic equilibrium and, abroad, into an uneasy truce with Moscow. The regime of Party leader Dubcek and Premier Cernik has, in effect, promised that it will control the pace of domestic reform; Moscow has gained the appearance of Czech compliance; but Prague seems at the same time to have been able to preserve the essential substance of its democratic experiment.

---

* This memorandum was produced solely by CIA. It was prepared by the Office of National Estimates and coordinated with the Office of Current Intelligence.

GROUP I
Excluded from automatic downgrading and declassification

S-E-C-R-E-T

Approved For Release 2006/12/11 : CIA-RDP79R00967A000800010004-9

S-E-C-R-E-T

2. The compromise seems to have come about, sequentially, as a result of strong Soviet pressures, rising Czech concern, mildly concessionary Czech responses, and, finally, the Soviets' own anxiety to find some way to avoid direct military intervention. It is true, nonetheless, that if quiescence has been restored to the relationship, it is by no means assured indefinitely. An undetermined number of Soviets are currently engaged in a Warsaw Pact exercise on Czech soil; their presence serves, at a minimum, as an ominous reminder to the Dubcek regime of Soviet power and of the USSR's continuing interest in Czech developments. The recently concluded plenum of the Czechoslovak Central Committee was reassuring to the Soviets in some respects but not at all in others. Dubcek, in fact, is working both sides of the street. He is trying to buy off Moscow with promises of continued Communist authority in Czechoslovakia and unswerving Czech loyalty to the Warsaw Pact. At the same time, he is seeking to strengthen his domestic position by pledging at least the gradual growth of democracy at home and independence abroad.

S-E-C-R-E-T

The Soviet-Czechoslovak Crisis Unfolds

Approved For Release 2007/03/13 : CIA-RDP79B00887A000500010051-5

S-E-C-R-E-T

25X1

CENTRAL INTELLIGENCE AGENCY

OFFICE OF NATIONAL ESTIMATES

10 May 1968

SPECIAL MEMORANDUM NO. 10-68

SUBJECT: The Crisis in Soviet-Czechoslovak Relations*

SUMMARY

During the last week or so Soviet concern over developments in Czechoslovakia has clearly been increasing at a rapid rate. We believe that the Soviets have issued a serious warning to Prague to arrest its wayward course, and that, if this proves ineffective, Moscow intends to use additional sanctions. The best judgment that can be made at this stage is that the Soviets will probably stop short of military intervention. But the stakes for the Soviet leaders are high, and such a move can no longer be excluded.

* * * * * * * * * * * *

---

* This memorandum was produced solely by CIA. It was prepared by the Office of National Estimates and coordinated with the Office of Current Intelligence.

GROUP 1
Excluded from automatic
downgrading and
declassification

S-E-C-R-E-T

Approved For Release 2007/03/13 : CIA-RDP79B00887A000500010051-5

25X1

S-E-C-R-E-T

1. The Soviet leadership, after several months of fretting, fuming, and temporizing, seems now to have decided that heavy pressures will be needed to push the alarmingly wayward Czechs back into line. Signs of this from Moscow, Prague, and elsewhere have begun to accumulate at a startling rate. In the last day or two there has been evidence of some Soviet troop movements in Poland and East Germany toward Czechoslovak frontiers. Chances of at least an open political clash of some sort between the two countries, or of an open clash between contending forces within Czechoslovakia, or of both, thus seem to be increasing, and rapidly so.

The Moscow Meetings

2. Precisely what took place during Alexander Dubcek's hurried trip to Moscow last weekend remains a mystery. A Czech source's description of the meetings as "rough", however, seems plausible. The Soviet leaders, who were inclined initially to view post-Novotny political developments in Czechoslovakia as "revisionist", are said to see them now -- as did Ulbricht from the very beginning -- as "counterrevolutionary." (A similar change in Soviet terminology took place in October 1956 vis-a-vis Hungary.) The subsequent quick convocation in Moscow of the four Eastern

S-E-C-R-E-T

TOP SECRET

25X1

CENTRAL INTELLIGENCE AGENCY
Directorate of Intelligence
12 July 1968

INTELLIGENCE MEMORANDUM

The Czechoslovak-Soviet Struggle

Summary

Soviet-Czech relations are again at a point of high tension. Moscow has publicly likened the situation in Czechoslovakia today to that which existed in Hungary just before the revolt there twelve years ago. The message, though implicit, was clear to all: Soviet troops which were moved into Czechoslovakia were placed there not for the "exercises" that provided a pretext, but as a token of Moscow's readiness to intervene militarily if worst came to worst. The Soviets have not been persuaded by Dubcek's repeated assurances that he can control the situation, and they have not seen the course of liberalization he has set in train slowed or changed. They have, therefore, been in no hurry to withdraw the forces they have positioned in his country.

For their part, the Czech leaders seem not to have lost their nerve. Indeed, their resolve seems to have stiffened under Soviet pressure. There is little choice for them but to stand their ground on the key issues. They seem to understand more clearly than their Soviet overlords that what has been set in motion in Czechoslovakia will not easily be reversed.

Note: This memorandum was produced solely by CIA. It was prepared jointly by the Office of Current Intelligence and the Office of Strategic Research and coordinated with the Office of National Estimates.

TOP SECRET

25X1

1. There is no longer any pretense that the Soviet units that arrived in Czechoslovakia in mid-June for what the Czechs once hopefully billed as a standard communications exercise were departing gracefully and on time. It is now a matter of the Czechoslovaks "negotiating" their removal.

2. Some of the foreign forces have been withdrawn--the Czechoslovak minister of defense uses the figure 35 percent--but Soviet ground force elements in unknown numbers, as well as aircraft and tanks, remain. They may all go in the near future. On the other hand, the Russians may try to keep a military presence in Czechoslovakia until such time as they feel easier about political trends within the country. Or the units that participated in the June exercises may be pulled out, but only temporarily. The Soviet commander of the Warsaw Pact is said already to have proposed that another "exercise" be held in Czechoslovakia next month. The Russians may devise yet other forms of military pressure.

The Soviet View

3. While these questions remain, there can no longer be any question that the Warsaw Pact, to which Prague has repeatedly affirmed its allegiance, is one of Moscow's chosen instruments of leverage with the Czechoslovaks. Under its cover, the Soviets, in a real sense, have already intervened militarily in Czechoslovakia. It is also clear that, in their undulating course, Soviet-Czechoslovak relations are again at a point of high tension.

4. This has been the pattern of relations ever since the old order in Prague was overthrown in January, and unless the Czechoslovak regime lurches more sharply to the left or right than it has yet done, this pattern may persist for some time. Moscow must realize that it cannot turn the clock back in Czechoslovakia, even if it wanted to. But the Soviets want greater certainty than they now have that the new order in Prague is stabilizing, is master in its own house, and has the will and the way to force internal political ferment to subside.

T-O-P S-E-C-R-E-T SC 05890-68

CENTRAL INTELLIGENCE AGENCY
OFFICE OF NATIONAL ESTIMATES

12 July 1968
1900 Hours

MEMORANDUM FOR THE DIRECTOR

SUBJECT: The Crisis in Czechoslovakia

1. Relations between Moscow and Prague have deteriorated to the lowest point since the change in the Czechoslovak leadership in January. The situation appears to be moving toward a decisive stage.

2. During the Warsaw Pact exercise in June, the Soviets introduced several thousand military personnel into Czechoslovakia. The bulk of these remain in the country, concentrated northwest and northeast of Prague. Western military attache sightings have not confirmed the presence of such large numbers of Soviet troops. Some four to six divisions have apparently been moved into positions in close proximity to the Czechoslovak frontier. The number of Soviet troops which have actually entered the country cannot be determined.

GROUP 1
Excluded from automatic
downgrading and
declassification

T-O-P S-E-C-R-E-T

T-O-P S-E-C-R-E-T   SC 05890-68

3. Since about 10 July five new communications links controlled by the Soviet General Staff have been established: two terminals appear to be located in Czechoslovakia; a third is located near Budapest; another is near Uzhgorod on the Soviet-Czechoslovak border; the last is southwest of Magdeburg, East Germany. These additional links indicate an expectation by the Soviets of a substantial increase in communications. The establishment of these terminals suggests, though it does not prove, a movement or preparations for a movement of Soviet troops into Czechoslovakia from the USSR, Hungary, and East Germany

4. Within the last two weeks increased propaganda indicates that Moscow has made some new decisions regarding Czechoslovakia. On 27 June the "2000 Words" Declaration of the Czechoslovak liberals (many of them Communist Party members) was published in several Czechoslovak newspapers. On 30 June TASS announced that the Warsaw Pact exercise was ended, then cancelled the announcement a few hours later. In early July Moscow, Warsaw, Pankow, Budapest, and Sofia sent private letters to Prague, apparently warning the Czechoslovak Party leadership and summoning the Czechs to a meeting; the Dubcek regime refused to attend. On 11 July Pravda attacked the "2000 Words" Declaration as being

- 2 -

T-O-P S-E-C-R-E-T

T-O-P S-E-C-R-E-T   SC 05890-68

"counterrevolutionary," and in the spirit of the "counter-revolutionary elements" who "attempted to undermine the Hungarian people's socialist achievements" in 1956. The most ominous part of the article is that it judges guilty by association "certain leading figures in Czechoslovakia" who have made "ambiguous statements in which they try to minimize the danger inherent in the counterrevolutionary '2000 Words'." This probably points to Dubcek himself.

5. The heightened Soviet pressure constitutes a demand on Dubcek to halt or reverse the basic current of political evolution in Czechoslovakia since last January. They are backing up this demand with an evident threat of military force. To satisfy the Soviets now, Dubcek would have to make some visible concession, such as the reimposition of press censorship; or the arrest of the authors of the "2000 Words;" or the purge of some of Dubcek's liberal associates who have been criticized by the Soviet press, such as Cisar or Kriegel; or his acquiescence in the permanent stationing of some foreign troops on Czechoslovak soil. It would be extremely difficult for Dubcek to make any of these concessions at this point without running a serious risk of public disorder, with a strong anti-Soviet cast. Thus the most recent developments

- 3 -

T-O-P S-E-C-R-E-T

T-O-P S-E-C-R-E-T SC 05890-68

indicate that the chances for a violent Soviet intervention have sharply increased.

FOR THE BOARD OF NATIONAL ESTIMATES:

ABBOT SMITH
Chairman

-4-

T-O-P S-E-C-R-E-T

Approved For Release 2009/04/21 : CIA-RDP94T00754R000200290004-5

TOP SECRET

25X1

CENTRAL INTELLIGENCE AGENCY
Directorate of Intelligence
2 August 1968

INTELLIGENCE MEMORANDUM

Military Developments in the Soviet-Czech Confrontation

Summary

Soviet military pressure against Czechoslovakia has grown steadily as the political confrontation has intensified. Within the last two weeks five field armies have been poised near Czech borders, Soviet tactical air forces near Czechoslovakia have been increased 70 percent, and large Soviet troop units have been seen moving inside Czechoslovakia.

Soviet troop activity in May and June appeared to be mainly a show of force. This troop activity had limited value as a genuine threat of large-scale intervention because the units involved were in a peacetime configuration and lacked the support elements necessary for extended combat.

In mid-July, however, the pressure tactics entered a new phase. The Soviets began a major call-up of civilian reservists and vehicles in the western USSR --an unprecedented move for them in peacetime--necessary to support deployments in Eastern Europe. The evidence, however, does not suggest any extensive mobilization of low-strength divisions.

The full scope of the Soviet mobilization is not known, but by now it could have provided a control and support structure sufficient to support a doubling of Soviet ground forces strength in Eastern Europe.

Note: This memorandum was produced solely by CIA. It was prepared by the Office of Strategic Research.

TOP SECRET

25X1

Approved For Release 2009/04/21 : CIA-RDP94T00754R000200290004-5

Military Events

1. As the Soviet-Czech confrontation has intensified, the Soviets have increasingly relied on the threat of military intervention to deter Czech resistance. The Czech armed forces, in contrast, have not shown any indications of preparing for hostilities.

2. In early May the Soviets moved a few divisions to positions near the Czech border. In mid-June elements of these divisions, tactical air units, and high-level staffs entered Czechoslovakia under the guise of a Warsaw Pact exercise. Most of these units subsequently left.

3. In mid-July the Soviet pressure tactics entered a new phase. On 23 July the Soviet press reported extensive mobilization of men and equipment throughout the western USSR as part of a large rear services exercise. Moscow later announced that the exercise had been extended to East Germany and Poland.

4. Soviet, Polish, and East German forces were subsequently massed in areas near the Czech border. By 30 July five armies were known to have been poised against Czechoslovakia, and there have been indications of further reinforcement from the USSR (see map). In addition, tactical air forces near the Czech border have been increased from 14 to 24 regiments.

5. On 31 July large Soviet units--at least one division--were sighted in central Czechoslovakia.

6. In short, it appears that the Soviet high command has in about two weeks' time completed military preparations sufficient for intervening in Czechoslovakia if that is deemed necessary by the political leadership. (For a detailed chronology of events, see Annex.)

Approved For Release 2009/04/21 : CIA-RDP94T00754R000200290004-5
TOP SECRET   25X1

                         25X1

Mobilization

7. In developing this military posture, the Soviets and their Polish and East German allies have mobilized to a degree unprecedented in peacetime, despite the danger of provoking counteractions by the West and destabilizing the military situation in Central Europe.

                         25X1

9. Existing combat units at the division or army level are not, by themselves, capable of sustained military activity. The Warsaw Pact forces are structured so that only the front-level organization is capable of sustained independent action, with the facility for continuous re-supply of the combat units. By design, the line divisions and, to a large degree, the armies have only combat responsibilities and rely on the front and the front rear services for the bulk of their logistic requirements. Effective employment of the combat elements is contingent upon the early establishment of a functioning rear services organization. Although individual divisions can be moved over long distances prior to mobilization, they cannot fight for more than a few days without this support.

10. Except for the Soviet forces in Germany, Soviet ground forces have little front organization or functioning rear services elements in peacetime. Front staff and headquarters elements are submerged

- 3 -
TOP SECRET   25X1
Approved For Release 2009/04/21 : CIA-RDP94T00754R000200290004-5

in the peacetime military administrative structure without identity as an existing operational force. The service units are at low or cadre strength and are only concerned with the routine day-to-day supply and maintenance of a garrisoned army.

11. the Soviets have carried out many of the steps needed for mobilization. A vital feature of the exercise was the announced mobilization of reservists and civilian vehicles. The Soviets later announced that the exercise had been expanded to include Polish and East German armed forces. While we are unable to confirm the scope of the Soviet mobilization, the announcements clearly imply that it is of major proportions. Such an effort could by now be sufficient to support a doubling of Soviet army strength in Eastern Europe. There is no evidence, however, of any extensive mobilization of low-strength Soviet divisions.

12. According to Warsaw Pact plans, mobilization begins with the alerting of key command and control personnel and their separation from the peacetime administrative structure. Reservists and civilians must be called up and integrated in the required units. Some men and vehicles will be used to augment reduced-strength combat elements, with the great majority used to create the rear service units. Some supply units are at low strength and can be filled out by adding the required mix of men and vehicles. Other units must be created entirely from mobilized resources. Many civilian transportation organizations are mobilized with no more than minor modification of their existing organizational structure. Concurrently with these steps, the rail transportation system for westward movement must be geared up and much of the available rolling stock assembled at unit areas and at border transshipment points.

13. In the current buildup, Polish rail cars reportedly began to be massed about 23 July. Further evidence suggests that Soviet forces from the Baltic and Belorussian Military Districts began entering Poland about 28 July. Forces from these areas

heretofore have not been involved with Czechoslovakia. This movement approximates expected actions of the Soviet Union in the event of a reinforcement against NATO. It is possible that because of the shift of three GSFG armies towards Czechoslovakia, the Soviets feel a need to fill the void created in their defenses against NATO.

14. Warsaw Pact procedures allow movement to begin before all the units are created or brought up to strength since the front is designed for phased deployment. Deployment involves moving the units by road or trains in such order that they arrive with organizational integrity. The numbers of men and vehicles involved, combined with the complexity of the routing and scheduling, require a high degree of control and maximum utilization of the transportation network for a successful and timely operation. Once the front is organized and the transportation network made available, about four divisions per day or approximately one army could be moved from the western USSR through Poland.

The Threat

[redacted] units have redeployed southward within East Germany to the area closest to western Czechoslovakia, where the eight full-strength Czech divisions are located.

16. The Polish field army from the Silesian Military District has been reoriented toward the Czechoslovak border. At least one Soviet army from the Carpathian Military District is partially deployed inside Czechoslovakia.

17. Military attache observations indicate that the Soviet Southern Group of Forces in Hungary is out of garrison and that its four divisions are now close to the Czech frontier.

Anticipating Surprise
The Soviets Invade

APPROVED FOR RELEASE
DATE: SEP 2004

~~SECRET~~

EO 12958 3.3(b)(1)>25Yrs
(a)

SC No. 08380/68

CENTRAL INTELLIGENCE AGENCY
Directorate of Intelligence
20 August 1968

INTELLIGENCE MEMORANDUM

Military Intervention in Czechoslovakia

1. About 2300 hours, local time Prague, (1800 hours EDT) on 20 August, Soviet, Polish, East German, Hungarian and Bulgarian troops began moving into Czechoslovakia, according to a Prague radio broadcast. Prague radio stated that the troops were moving into Czechoslovakia without the knowledge of Czechoslovak party and government leaders.

2. At 2145 hours, Prague radio appealed to all citizens to maintain calm and to offer no resistance to the troops moving into the country. According to the broadcast no commands had been issued to Czechoslovak military forces to defend the country. In Prague, the National Assembly (parliament) and the party central committee immediately assembled. They apparently are still in session.

SECRET

4. There have been, as yet, no indications of ground forces movements into Czechoslovakia, but it is likely that deployment occurred from assembly positions in Czechoslovakia's borders in East Germany, Poland, the USSR, and Hungary. At least 25 divisions had been deployed in these areas for several weeks. As recently as three days ago they had rehearsed a plan to move into western Czechoslovakia.

5. A member of the Soviet delegation to the UN has stated that the Soviet government and its Warsaw Pact allies were intervening militarily in Czechoslovakia at the request of the Czechoslovak government. Otherwise, there has been no official Soviet statement, either as to the act of intervention or as to the pretext on which the action is based.

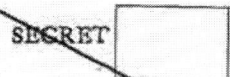

6. According to a press report from London, telephone contact between Britain and the Soviet Union was cut soon after Prague Radio's announcement of intervention.

7. The Soviet intervention came hard on reports of the convening of an extraordinary session of the Soviet Central Committee. Soviet leaders interrupted their vacations in order to attend the session, according to these reports. This sequence suggests that the Soviet leadership was seeking the last-minute approval of the Central Committee for a decision which had already been made. The circumstances raise the possibility that the decision resulted from a rebellion within the Politburo against policies which, in recent weeks, have appeared to put the USSR on the short end in the Soviet-Czechoslovak conflict.

~~CONFIDENTIAL~~

CENTRAL INTELLIGENCE AGENCY
Directorate of Intelligence
21 August 1968

MEMORANDUM

SUBJECT: The Soviet Decision to Intervene in Czechoslovakia

1. Between the end of the Cierna-Bratislava meetings and yesterday's invasion nothing happened inside Czechoslovakia to support Moscow's claim that these meetings were a great victory for Communist orthodoxy. Neither was there a notable recrudescence in Czechoslovakia of the "anti-socialist" trends which brought on the Warsaw meeting and its harsh ultimatum. Thus, we doubt that a rising sense of alarm in Moscow is the essential explanation for Soviet intervention.

2. The Soviet politburo on its return to Moscow did not summon the Central Committee to report on the Cierna and Bratislava meetings, but instead issued a communique in the name of the entire politburo saying that those meetings were a good piece of work. The Soviet leaders seem shortly thereafter to have scattered for their usual summer holidays. The Soviet press stood down its attacks on Czechoslovakia. The appearance given was that Moscow was willing at least to give the Czechs--presumably chastened by the nearness of their approach to the brink--a respite. What went on in Czechoslovakia during the short span of time since Cierna proved only that the Czechs had not understood Cierna to mean that they should put their reform movement into reverse.

3. It is not likely that the Soviets, even though they have persistently underestimated the strength of reformist spirit in Czechoslovakia expected miracles to be done by Dubcek in three weeks' time. Even if Dubcek had promised them, there was no chance he could deliver. What, then, brought the Russians, after they had decided to

~~CONFIDENTIAL~~

~~CONFIDENTIAL~~

step back at Cierna, to give the signal yesterday to crush the Czechoslovaks?

4. It may be some time before we can answer this question with any assurance. On the strength of what we know now, the most likely explanation appears to be that, under the impact of internal pressures within the leadership and of importuning from its anxious allies in Eastern Europe, the Soviet decision at Cierna to give Dubcek and company more time became unravelled. This would suppose—as there seems some reason to suppose—that the Soviet politburo when it went to Cierna was divided in mind, and that the standoff reached there derived mostly from Soviet irresolution. The fragile balance in the Soviet leadership which produced the Cierna agreement has, in the space of less than three weeks, been upset in favor of those who may all along have wanted the toughest kind of policy and have made use of the time and developments since Cierna to undo the agreement.

5. If, indeed, the political scales in Moscow have been in such precarious balance, it would not have needed a great shock to upset them, but only the absence of solid signs that developments in Prague were going Moscow's way. There were few of these. In the short time available to Dubcek his efforts to demonstrate that he could insure the unquestioned domination of the Communist party had not been impressive. Czechoslvak information media remained unruly and unrepentant. There was no indication that non-Communist political elements—for example, the Club of Committed Non-Party People and the revived Socialist party—were being forced to take cover. Despite the renewed pledges of fidelity to CEMA given at Cierna, there continued to be much talk in Prague of broader economic ties with the West.

6. The visits to Prague of Tito and Ceausescu were all too visible reminders that the ranks of independent Communist states were swelling. And, finally, with preparations moving ahead rapidly for the party congress scheduled to open on 9 September, it was becoming clear that the congress

-2-

~~CONFIDENTIAL~~

~~CONFIDENTIAL~~

might sound the death knell over the Czechoslovak party conservatives, Moscow's last hope for a brake on reformism in Prague. The congress would have meant not a check on the momentum of the Czechoslovak reform movement, but its confirmation. In addition, the cost of maintaining the mobilization of massive intervention forces may have created pressures in the leadership to use these forces or disband them.

7. Despite the smoothness of the Soviet military operation in Czechoslovakia, a number of Soviet political actions suggest that the decision to execute the plan of intervention came at a fairly late stage. Among these were Dobrynin's approach to the President, the convening of the Central Committee in the midst of the top leaders' vacation, the flimsiness of the legal base for Soviet action, and the failure to surface quickly an alternative leadership in Prague. Thus it would appear that Soviet intervention in Czechoslovakia did not follow naturally from the Cierna meeting but represents, instead, a scrapping of the position arrived at there.

The Aftermath
Assessing Damage and Impact

Approved For Release 2005/12/24 : CIA-RDP79R00904A001400020006-1

SECRET

CENTRAL INTELLIGENCE AGENCY

OFFICE OF NATIONAL ESTIMATES

3 September 1968

MEMORANDUM FOR THE DIRECTOR

SUBJECT: The Consequences of Czechoslovakia

SUMMARY

It is still very early to assess all the likely consequences of the Soviet military move into Czechoslovakia. Quite obviously, arrangements between the USSR and Czechoslovakia are fragile, and the current relative calm within Czechoslovakia could be broken at any time by popular manifestations against the occupation forces. It now appears more likely, however, that the people will reluctantly accept the results of the Soviet-imposed Moscow compromise, which -- in exchange for the Soviets' conditional acceptance of the Dubcek leadership and for a vague Soviet promise someday to withdraw the occupying forces -- commits Prague to renewed fealty to the USSR abroad and to a return to more orthodox communist policies at home. Moscow thus seems to have accomplished its principal immediate aims, the reversal of Czechoslovakia's movement away from the Bloc, the collapse of the Czech experiment in a new form of liberal and independent socialism, and the erection of new barriers against the emergence of any Czech-like developments elsewhere in Eastern Europe.

Among the costs of such accomplishment for the USSR, however, are the potentially explosive political strains endured by the Soviet leadership; the probable strengthening of anti-Soviet nationalism among the peoples of Eastern Europe; the reinforcement of polycentrist trends within the Communist Parties of the international movement, especially in Western Europe; and -- despite Soviet hopes to the contrary -- the possible disruption of a variety of Soviet policies across the world.

GROUP 1
S-E-C-R-E-T   Excluded from automatic
                downgrading and
                declassification

Approved For Release 2005/12/24 : CIA-RDP79R00904A001400020006-1

S-E-C-R-E-T

1. Contrary to indications last week that Moscow was preparing to crack down hard on the Czechs and on the Dubcek leadership, the Soviets now appear to be giving the Czechs some opportunity to put their own house in order. The most virulent Soviet accusations against the Czechs have lately been muted and have been accompanied by praise of both Dubcek and Svoboda. This turnabout -- the third time the Soviet press has changed its line on Dubcek -- and other anomalies (including, first and most conspicuously, the apparent lack of any clear-cut occupation policy once the invasion had been completed) has suggested Soviet indecision or even serious disagreements within the Soviet leadership. The following discussion offers some notions on how things might go now inside Czechoslovakia, how the Soviets might view this process, what the circumstances might be within the Soviet leadership, and, finally, a very brief consideration of the possible impact of the Czech affair on general Soviet policy.

The Scene in Czechoslovakia

2. The Czechoslovak leaders surely did their best in Moscow, under extraordinarily difficult circumstances, to obtain an honorable settlement and the withdrawal of all Warsaw Pact troops from Czech soil. But Dubcek and his comrades -- with their

- 2 -

S-E-C-R-E-T

DRAFT 22 Nov 68

MEMORANDUM FOR THE DIRECTOR OF CENTRAL INTELLIGENCE

SUBJECT: Post Mortem on Czech Crisis

REFERENCE: USIB-D-28.1/5, 11 October 1968

1. In accordance with instructions contained in reference, the Strategic Warning Working Group (SWWG) received the post mortem reports on the Czech crisis prepared by CIA, DIA, NSA and INR, and reviewed them thoroughly. The CIA and DIA reports are studies in considerable detail of the intelligence coverage of the Czech crisis from January 1968 until after the invasion of Czechoslovakia on 20 August by Soviet and other Eastern European forces. The INR summary addresses some aspects of the crisis of particular concern to the State Department and the NSA report gives details of SIGINT coverage during this period. These four reports, taken together, present a thorough, comprehensive and very detailed review of all intelligence activities--collection, analysis and reporting--during the nine month period of developing crisis and final military intervention. The reports are so complete in themselves that no attempt was made to summarize them as a single document. A very brief summary of events and intelligence coverage thereof is attached as Annex A. The INR, CIA, DIA and NSA reports are attached in subsequent annexes.

2. In the final analysis intelligence coverage of this crisis was adequate up to the point of the decision to invade Czechoslovakia. The capabilities of the forces to carry out the invasion was clearly stated. The intention to invade was not known until after the fact. The lack of ability to assess more accurately the likelihood of this intention was the point of intelligence failure in the Czech crisis.

3. There are certain areas of possible improvement in intelligence performance which have been taken under consideration by the SWWG for possible referral to action agencies. These areas include:

25X1

4. The SWWG believes that the Soviet actions during the period of May-August 1968 offer an unique opportunity to study the procedures utilized by the USSR to conduct military operations. Seldom has a major military power made such a large-scale deployment of forces under non-wartime conditions which permit a study of the many facets revealed by those operations in something of an academic

25X1

atmosphere. Much more can be done with the evidence accumulated over the past few months than has been possible in these post mortem studies which have been prepared by busy people also occupied by on-going responsibilities. Consequently, we recommend an intensive further study of the evidence be made by an objective group. This study possibly could be achieved by the establishment of an ad hoc group established solely for the purpose and staffed by representatives from CIA, DIA, State, NSA and the military services. Alternatively, such a study might be undertaken under contract by a suitable existing research organization. Specific guidance for such a study would have to be developed and preparations of this guidance would be a major undertaking. The SWWG, if directed, could monitor the development of this guidance which would require major contributions from member agencies.

Chairman
Strategic Warning Working Group

DRAFT: 22 Nov 68

SUMMARY

The development of the Czech crisis was protracted, extending from January 5, 1968 when Dubcek replaced Novotny. The possibility of the impending crisis was recognized from its inception, with an initial report on January 11 of the beginning of far reaching changes in Czech life.

The intelligence community became increasingly concerned with and reported the growing ferment in Czech life and the impact this might have on other countries in Eastern Europe. On March 20 a recommendation was made to the Senior Interdepartmental Group that they take the implications of the situation under consideration. A State Department Task Force on Czechoslovakia was formed in April and NATO set up an intelligence watch with a special daily reporting procedure in May.

The confrontation at Dresden on March 23 between Dubcek and the leaders from the Soviet Union, East Germany, Poland, Hungary and Rumania was inconclusive and satisfied no one. A month later, on April 23, an intelligence memorandum reported that Dubcek's program had led to a bloodless but nevertheless very real revolution in Czechoslovakia and that Soviet and other leaders obviously feared the spread of these concepts to their own countries. It was recognized and reported by the intelligence analysts that this constituted a threat to vital Soviet interests and that if political pressures failed, the Soviets would face a choice between acceptance and military action.

Intelligence publications first began to suggest that a Soviet military intervention in Czechoslovakia was a real possibility in late March. This warning was repeated and on May 10 definite evidence of Soviet troop concentrations and maneuvers on the Czech border was reported for the first time.

Reporting on Soviet military preparations and maneuvers from May 10 on was thorough. Our reporting was able to make the important distinctions among the relatively small deployments for political purposes in May, the extensive deployments involved in the Warsaw Pact exercises in Czechoslovakia in June/July, and the very large deployments, complete with mobilization and reinforcement from the rear areas, which were undertaken from the second half of July and culminated in the actual invasion. Their capability to intervene in Czechoslovakia at any time should they elect to do so was clearly stated. However, it was not possible to report when the decision to invade was being taken, when the Soviet troops had received their orders and were preparing to move, or when the Soviet troops actually began to move.

Approved For Release 2006/02/01 : CIA-RDP80B01495R001300130019-7

SECRET

25X1   DRAFT: [ ] 22 Nov 68

SUMMARY

The development of the Czech crisis was protracted, extending from January 5, 1968 when Dubcek replaced Novotny. The possibility of the impending crisis was recognized from its inception, with an initial report on January 11 of the beginning of far reaching changes in Czech life.

The intelligence community became increasingly concerned with and reported the growing ferment in Czech life and the impact this might have on other countries in Eastern Europe. On March 20 a recommendation was made to the Senior Interdepartmental Group that they take the implications of the situation under consideration. A State Department Task Force on Czechoslovakia was formed in April and NATO set up an intelligence watch with a special daily reporting procedure in May.

The confrontation at Dresden on March 23 between Dubcek and the leaders from the Soviet Union, East Germany, Poland, Hungary and Rumania was inconclusive and satisfied no one. A month later, on April 23, an intelligence memorandum reported that Dubcek's program had led to a bloodless but nevertheless very real revolution

SECRET
Approved For Release 2006/02/01 : CIA-RDP80B01495R001300130019-7

ACKNOWLEDGEMENTS

CIA's Historical Collections Division gratefully acknowledges the following organizations for their courtesy in providing material for this collection.

ABC News VideoSource
125 West End Avenue
New York, NY 10023

CBS News Information Resources
524 West 57th Street
New York, NY 10019

Pacifica Radio Archives
3729 Cahuenga Boulevard, West
North Hollywood, CA 91604
www.pacificaradioarchives.org

The Herb Block Foundation
1730 M Street, NW
Washington, DC 20036

**The New York Times-PARS
International Corp.**
253 West 35th Street
New York, NY 10001

Time, Inc.
TimeReprints_US@time.com

Other Video, Audio, and Photographs provided by:
Lyndon B. Johnson Presidential Library Audiovisual Archives
2313 Red River Street
Austin, TX 78705

ABC and CBS News Video Clips Provided by:
Vanderbilt University Television News Archive
110 Twenty-first Avenue, South
Nashville, TN 37203

Music provided by:
Kevin MacLeod
www.incompetech.com

The complete bibliographic citations for all of the material provided by the above may be found on the DVD.

Made in United States
Orlando, FL
16 January 2022

13548609R00037